Looking After Our Rivers

By Cameron Macintosh

Our planet's rivers are amazing! They can flow down from high peaks and finish at the sea.

Rivers provide fresh water for people and animals.

Rivers are strong!
After decades and decades,
rivers can carve canyons through
the land.

Rivers are home to lots of wildlife.

Fish live in the water.

Other animals visit for a drink or to hunt in the rapids.

These animals have a talent for catching fish.

The soil around rivers is rich and fertile.

We can grow a large volume of crops in fertile soil.

Rivers provide fresh water for us to drink.

We make dams in rivers as a method for collecting fresh water. Then the water is cleaned and comes through our taps!

Rivers are beautiful places to visit.

You can float down the river
on a boat.
But first put on a life jacket!

I travel down this river with my mum and dad.

If we don't look after our rivers, they can get dirty and turn toxic.

Animals that live there can get sick and vanish.

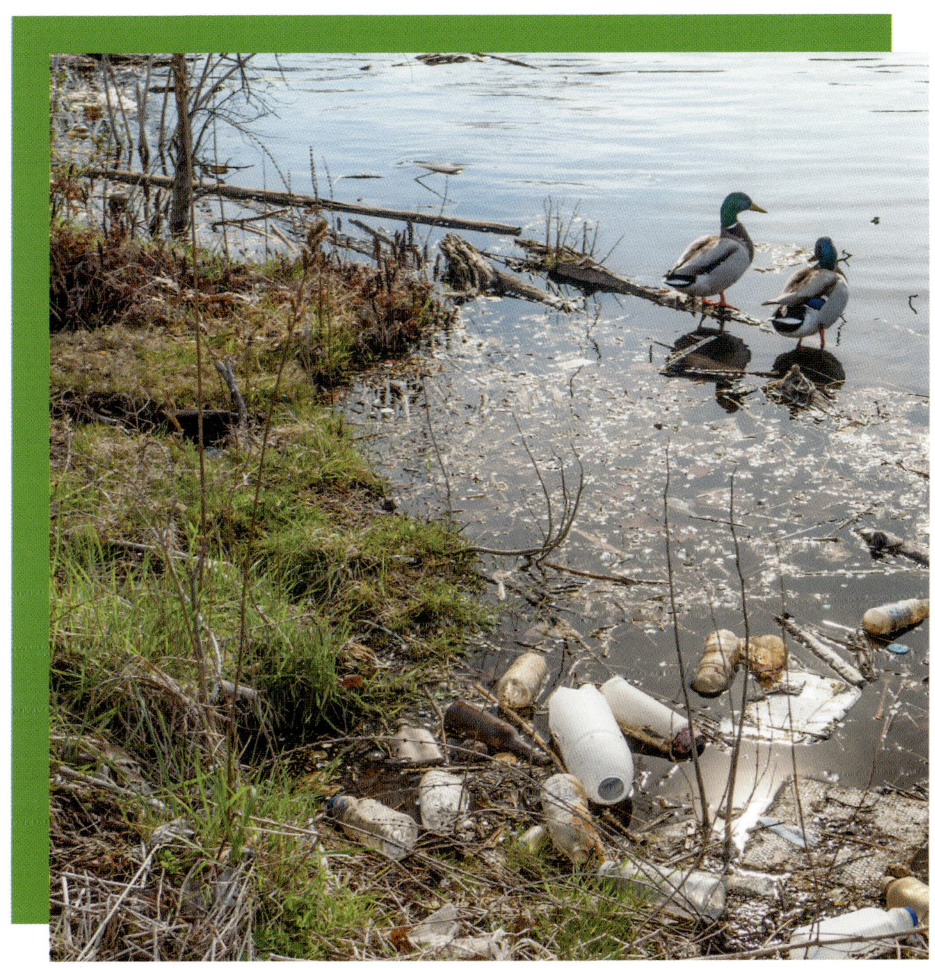

If we cut down trees, high levels of soil run into our rivers.

To limit this, we should plant trees along the banks of rivers.

We must clean rubbish from our rivers and not dump toxic waste into them.

When you visit a river, get into the habit of putting rubbish in a rubbish bin or in your pocket.

Never throw it in the river!

We all need to help protect our planet's beautiful rivers.

CHECKING FOR MEANING

1. What kind of water do rivers provide people and animals? *(Literal)*
2. What is the soil like around rivers? *(Literal)*
3. What would happen to drinking water if rivers turned toxic? *(Inferential)*
4. Why are rivers important for both plants and animals? *(Evaluative)*

EXTENDING VOCABULARY

canyon	What is a canyon? What words could you use to describe what it would be like inside a canyon?
toxic	Read the word *toxic*. What does it mean if something is toxic? What else could be described as toxic?
vanish	Read the word *vanish*. What does it mean if animals vanish from a place? What is the opposite of the word *vanish*?

MOVING BEYOND THE TEXT

1. Have you ever seen a river or been to a river? Describe your experience.
2. Why is it important to plant trees on riverbanks?
3. What are some animals that might live in or around rivers near you?
4. When have you had to work with others to protect or take care of something?

TIME TO WRITE

Write about some ways that people can protect or care for rivers. Say why it is important to do this.